RUNNING THROUGH THE RAIN

My Stories, Reflections, and Kind Reminders

T.W. Suggs

ISBN: 978-1-7369066-0-6

This book is dedicated to all of you.

I celebrate your strength, beauty, and resilience.

I celebrate you.

Contents

Introduction

I MAGINE YOU WERE going for a walk outside when, suddenly, the skies darkened, the clouds thickened, and the rain began to fall. Most of us would open an umbrella—or (if we didn't have an umbrella) a newspaper, trash bag, coats, or whatever we had—to shield ourselves from the rain. Even with an umbrella, most people would try to get out of the rain as quickly as possible to avoid getting wet.

This is similar to how many of us deal with our stories. Similar to rain, some of our stories can be cold, biting, and uncomfortable. We often run from them and open "umbrellas" so we don't have to feel them on our skin.

This book is a compilation of stories from my life. Some stories are difficult like "Hide and Seek" and others are sweet and warm like "Blow It Out Your ..." or "The Gromblewog." I also share Reflections and Kind

Reminders, which are gems we can take with us as we navigate this journey called life.

I fold my umbrella as I tell these stories, and I hope you feel encouraged to fold yours as well. It's one thing to be in the rain, but it's something else to feel it. Feel your rain and instead of running from it. You are able to run through it.

You are amazing, beautiful, and far more resilient than you could ever imagine. As you read these stories, I invite you to fold your umbrella and come with me so we can run through the rain.

Bowl Batter

"**N**ow, Tommie, keep the blender in the bowl. Okay, baby?"

"Okay, Mommy," I said. My entire six-year-old body trembled and vibrated as I tried to control the direction of the handheld blender and keep it in the bowl. The beige batter became smoother, and the lumps started disappearing.

"You got it?"

"Yes, I got it, Mom," I said with a huge smile.

"Now do that until the batter is nice and smooth," I heard her say over the sound of the whirling machine.

A few moments later she looked over my shoulder. "Okay, baby, that's good. Now we have to butter the bottom of the pan."

She cut a small pad of butter from our stick of butter and let it fall into the center of the pan. "Okay, now rub that butter all over the pan."

"With my hands?" I asked with my face squinched.

"Yeah, with your hands. You can wash them later."

My mom passed me the pan. I rubbed it with butter. It was like rubbing lotion on smooth, silver skin.

"I'm done!" I yelled out.

"Okay, good." She grabbed the pan and held it up to the light, tilting it from side to side to inspect my work. "You missed a spot."

I quickly filled that spot with rubbed-on butter.

"Now we need to pour the batter into this pan."

"Can I do it?" I shouted.

"Maybe next time. This is a big bowl, and it's heavy."

My mom poured the batter from the bowl into the pan. The batter slid out of the bowl and melted into itself in the pan. I looked on in amazement.

"Okay, all done. Now I'm going to put this in the oven, and we'll check on it in thirty minutes. No jumping or playing. Or the cake will fall."

Even though I had no idea what that meant, I knew that if I made it fall, I would get in trouble.

"You did a good job, sweetheart! Here."

My mom passed me the bowl. The reward for a job well done. Leftover batter. As I licked the bowl, enjoying the reward for my labor, the bowl swallowed my little head.

Who needs a cake when you have batter?

Hide and Seek

"ONE, TWO, THREE, four, five, six, seven, eight, nine ..."

It was April's turn to count while Barry and I hid. Her high-pitched six-year-old voice pierced through the entire neighborhood.

"Thirteen, fourteen, fifteen, sixteen, seventeen ..."

Only April, Barry, and I were playing. We all were around six years old. While April counted, Barry and I decided to hide together, but we couldn't agree where the best spot would be.

"Let's hide behind the tree!" I whispered.

"No, let's hide under the chair on my grandma's porch," Barry said. His breath was hot and smelled like banana Now and Laters.

I agreed.

During this time in my life, my mom and I lived

with my grandmother in the West Oak Lane section of Philadelphia. Barry's grandmother lived a few doors down.

We ran to his grandmother's porch and scurried beneath one of the long chairs, giggling because we found the perfect hiding space. "April will never find us under here," Barry said.

"Twenty-eight, twenty-nine, thirty! Ready or not, here I come!" She belted out.

Our giggling quieted so we wouldn't be heard or seen by April. I could tell she was having a hard time finding us because it felt like forever while we were laying there.

More time had passed, and April still hadn't found us. While I was laying there, contemplating coming out from beneath the porch chair to find April, I felt something wet on the back of my neck. I shrugged and moved a bit further from Barry, who was laying behind me, but just enough to keep from being seen by April. A few moments later, I felt it again. It was Barry's lips. He was kissing the back of my neck. "Stop, Barry." I wiped the wetness off and continued hiding. I felt the wetness again. Barry was still kissing and touching me in places my mom told me no one should touch. I knew it was wrong, but I wasn't sure how to respond. My six years on this planet didn't provide me with a point of reference for what was happening or what to do. I heard a faint voice calling my name. It was my grandmother. I popped from beneath the porch chair and did my best to tuck in my shirt, button my pants, and fasten my belt. I didn't want anyone to know what had just happened. In fact, I didn't really know what had just happened. I ran down steps and down the street to where my grandmother was standing in front of our house. A neighbor saw Barry and me beneath his grandmother's porch chair and told my grandmother, who gave me a thorough scolding. My mom wasn't home, but when she got home, my grandmother told her what the neighbor saw. My mom and I had a long talk. I don't remember everything she said, but I remember it being a long talk and her telling me to never do that again.

This day changed my life. It was the day that Barry introduced me to a friend I never knew he had—trauma.

First impressions are everything.

Reflection
Debt Collectors

"Hɪ. Tʜɪs ɪs not an attempt to collect a debt. Any information collected during this call will not be used for that purpose. I forgive you."

A Father's Pride, A Son's Shame

ONE SPRING DAY in my sixth-grade year, our social studies teacher had just given us an assignment to complete after a long lecture.

"Okay, everyone, for the rest of our time together in class, we'll be using our textbooks. Read pages 117 to 119 and answer the questions at the bottom of page 119." When we heard the assignment, the entire class started to complain, which Mr. Berk cut short.

"Okay, okay, enough of the complaining. I'm trying to give you work now so I don't have to give you homework this weekend."

Almost all at the same time, our eyes lit up at the thought of having a weekend free of homework. Excited at the idea of having a free weekend, we quickly busied ourselves with the assignment. Our pencils twirled and zigged and zagged on our papers as we wrote our answers down in our marble notebooks.

While I was working on my assignment, I noticed a figure moving by in the hallway in my peripheral vision. I was able to see everything that happened in the hallway because my desk was next to the door. Though the door was closed, it had a window, so it was easy to see into the hallway. I didn't think much of it, so I continued to work on my assignment, still excited at the idea of having a homework-free weekend. The figure passed by the door again. I looked up to see who it was, but they had vanished. I moved on to the next question. "A _____ is a landform with a high elevation and more or less level surface." While I tried to figure out what was supposed to go in the blank, I started to hear a few of the kids laughing under their breath. I looked over at Tyler to see what was so funny. He said, "Isn't that your dad?" as he pointed at the door. When I looked over, it *was* my dad. He was the figure that kept walking back and forth in the hallway. He was trying to find my classroom but had a difficult time finding it. He was wearing his dark green work uniform and looked like he had just finished a big project. He came to bring my lunch, which I had left at home. He stared at me with a smile.

I lowered my eyes and continued to do my classwork, and I pretended I didn't know him. I was embarrassed. Other kids' parents wore nice clothes when they came to see them. My dad wore janitor clothes. I saw out of the side of my eye that a teacher walked by. My dad handed my lunch to the teacher and asked him to give it to me. Right before my dad disappeared from the window, I looked up again to see if he was still there. He was. But his face was different. The smile he wore proudly a few moments ago faded and was replaced by eyes that held hurt because he knew why I didn't acknowledge him. I'm sorry, dad.

Saturday Morning

THE MORNING SUNLIGHT dances on his brown face. His complexion looks like honey.

Golden rays sneak between the blinds in his window, jump on his bed, and splash their light on his white bedroom walls.

The ambient sound of his momma and poppa talking over the faint buzz of the television while pots and pans full of grits, eggs, and bacon slide and clang on the hot stove. The salty smell of bacon momma picked up from the Italian Market on Ninth Street and soft biscuits fills the air of his small bedroom.

His eyes are closed, but he is wide awake, hearing and smelling everything going on in the world around him.

Grinning like the cat that ate the canary, he stretches and twists and stretches. His arms fully extend, and his toes spread out, and he stretches. He turns over like his mama's flapjacks. Eyes still shut.

His door creaks open, and a head pops in. It's his momma checking on him. The sunlight makes her complexion like honey too. He pretends to be asleep.

She smiles. Her head disappears behind the door.

This is perfect. This is home. This is Saturday.

The New Kid

I T WAS 12:00 p.m. when the bell rang, and my math class had just ended. The bell actually didn't ring. It had more of an annoying heavy buzz sound that filled the rooms and echoed throughout the hallways. It was lunchtime! I began to grin at the thought of the peanut butter and jelly sandwich my mom made for me that morning. I packed my homework and textbooks into my bookbag, struggling to zip it closed because it was already overstuffed. My teacher was still speaking, but whatever she was saying didn't matter because the bell rang. I joined the herd of students piling and yelling at the door, squeezing through the narrow doorway to get out. "Don't forget, your book reports are due next Monday!" my teacher tried shouting over the sound of excited and hungry students. No one was really listening. It was time for lunch. Lunch was almost like Christmas. Most of the kids didn't prepare their own lunches. Instead, their parents prepared their lunch for them, so usually, they never knew what they were having for lunch until lunchtime. Other kids received lunch from the school. It was always the same thing. Pizza was always served on Friday. The rest of the week, kids had a piece of meat or nuggets, peas, mashed potatoes, and tater tots. I never got lunch from school.

I ran down to the lunchroom and walked into a room full of screaming and laughing kids. Peas flew through the air, and someone slingshotted a spoonful of mashed potatoes across the room. The lunchroom staff was yelling, trying to get the kids to sit down.

The lunchroom was the same place we had gym. Right before lunch, the staff would unfold the long tables that had a long bench to each side of them. They were ugly, hard, and dark brown with black trim. I stood in the doorway trying to find a place where I could sit. The scent of old lunch food was strong.

I saw an open spot at one of the tables in the back that seemed open. I was getting ready to walk there until I saw a kid sitting at a lunch table by himself on the other side of the lunchroom. I could tell he was a new kid because I had never seen him around and he was sitting by himself. He didn't seem bothered that he was eating by himself. I was hesitant about walking across the battlefield of kids, teachers, and flying food because I didn't know what the other kids would say if they saw me speaking with him. I already didn't fit in. The last thing I needed was for something to further destroy my nonexistent reputation. But I wanted to see who this new kid was. I mustered up some courage and made my way across the room to where he was sitting. As I stood in front of him, he shifted his focus from his lunch and looked at me. It was silent for a few seconds. I had a plan to make it across the lunchroom but didn't think about what I would say when I got there. He looked like a normal kid. His sneakers were a little worn like mine. I could see them as he swung his feet beneath the table playfully back and forth as he ate his lunch. He didn't seem too nerdy or mean like a bully. He seemed like a normal kid.

"Hi," I said nervously.

"Hi," he said back. It got quiet again. The noise of the kids screaming and playing in the background seemed to get louder.

I broke the silence. "You new here?" I asked awkwardly.

"Yeah. I started today."

"Oh, okay."

"Well, my name is Tommie. What's your name?" I asked.

He said, "My name is God."

God loves tater tots.

Preposition

"Now, a preposition is a word that shows time, direction, or location, and it comes before a noun. Words like *at, by, of, to,* or *on* are examples of prepositions." Ms. Eugene says as she scribbles the word *preposition* on the ashy green chalkboard in large white letters.

"Tommie, are you paying attention?"

I hate Ms. Eugene. She has such a deep voice. She sounds like a man.

The Fresh Prince

M Y FAMILY HAD just moved into our new home in West Oak Lane, an area in Philadelphia. Up until this point, we had been living with my grandmother, who lived in another part of West Oak Lane. It was only a fifteen-minute walk to get to her house. Our new first-floor, shotgun-style duplex was small, but it was ours. All the rooms in the apartment were in a line. First was the living room. Behind the living room was the kitchen. Behind the kitchen was the bathroom. Behind the bathroom was my small room. Behind my small room was my mom and dad's room.

I was still getting used to the new neighborhood and the new school. New classmates, new neighbors I have never met. I got lost easily walking home from school for the first week or so but learned my way around the neighborhood eventually.

I had just finished my homework and was ready to

watch television in the living room. I turned on one of my favorite shows, *The Fresh Prince of Bel-Air*. It was a sitcom about a black family who took in Will Smith, a young man trying to navigate life in a new world, Bel Air. I think I may have connected with Will on a deeper level. He grew up in a rough part of Philadelphia and was trying to find his way as a young black man. Just like me.

I caught the show at my favorite part, the opening theme music.

"In West Philadelphia born and raised. On the playground was where I spent most of my days ..."

I bobbed my head side to side as I chanted along with the theme music.

"When a couple of guys who were up to no good started making trouble in my neighborhood ..."

My mom was in the kitchen, making dinner and washing dishes.

Ssssss.

She had breaded another porkchop and dropped it in the hot grease, which popped and fizzled. The smell was making me even more hungry. The show was getting ready to come on when suddenly I heard what sounded like thunder rolling around on the porch. It was a posse of kids stampeding to my door. The thunder was followed by loud banging on the door. My mom answered.

"Hey, guys. How can I help you?

One of the kids spoke up. "Hi, Miss. We heard another kid moved here. Can he come out and play?"

My mom and I had just moved to the area the previous week, so I wasn't familiar with any of the kids who lived there.

"Oh, that's nice. Sure, I'll go get him." My eyes rolled to the back of my head. The last thing I needed was for something to separate me from Hillary, Carlton, and Will.

"Tommie, you have company at the door."

I reluctantly walked to the door to see six or seven little brown faces staring at me. My mom walked away to tend to dinner. I walked out on the porch, closing the door behind me to meet my unwanted guests.

"What's your name?" one of them asked.

"My name is Tommie."

"Tommie?" He frowned his face because in the hood there aren't many Tommies. There are a lot of Maliks, Jamals, Anthonys, Seans, and Tyriks, but never Tommies. This moment reminded me of why I hated my name.

"Is that your real name?" Some of the other kids on the porch giggled.

"Yes, that's my real name."

"Oh, okay, cool. Well, my name is Sean. That's Rob, Kyle, Marcus, Tiffany, April, and Jamal."

"Sup."

The guys said sup back, which is short for "what's up?" It's another way of saying hi.

The girls whispered and giggled.

"Can you come out and play? We're about to play Throw Up. You throw a ball up in the air, and whoever catches it has to run to base to win"

"Nah, I can't. I have homework I have to do." I was lying.

"Oh, okay, cool. Well, if you get done early, come outside."

"A'ight, cool."

"Cool."

They ran off the porch louder than how they came to play their game. I went back inside to finish watching *Fresh Prince*.

I wondered if Jazz was thrown out of the house yet.

Voices

IT WAS A cold and snowless night during the winter. Our breath could be seen against the blackness of night and was carried off by the evening wind. My mom had just picked me up from my aunt's house, who watched me over the weekend. She didn't live in a horrible part of the city, but it wasn't as nice as Cheltenham or Mt. Airy where they had lawns that were mowed, nice big homes with porches, and clean streets. My aunt's neighborhood wasn't as clean and had a few alley cats that wandered around. From time to time, you would also hear police sirens.

Usually, I had a great time at my aunt's house. When my mom would pick me up, I would tell her about my weekend, what we ate, the scary movies we watched, and the places we visited. This time, something was different. We scurried quickly to the car, leaving the faint white trail of our breath behind us. I tucked my hands deep in my pockets to keep them warm. I left my gloves on my desk at school. My mom unlocked my door first, and then she scuttled to the driver's side, unlocked her door, and got in the car. "Mmm, it's cold out there," she said under her breath. As I sat there in the passenger seat with my mom trying to find the right key to put into the ignition, tears started falling.

My mom was in the driver's seat, busy still trying to get the key into the ignition. She didn't see the tears falling. I broke my silence.

"Mom?"

"Yes, baby?" The keys jangled as she continued to find the keyhole on the side of the steering wheel.

"I hear voices."

The jangling stopped, and for a brief moment, it was completely silent. She turned to look at me. I could see the look of worry and confusion on her face.

"You hear voices? What are they saying to you?" she asked softly.

I cried harder. I was afraid and embarrassed. I knew that hearing voices wasn't normal, and I didn't know how to deal with hearing them. I knew that something about this was dark, and sharing it made me feel vulnerable and exposed. She unbuckled her seatbelt, reached over the armrest that was between us, and held me. The nearby yellow streetlight was our only source of light.

"Baby, what do you hear them saying to you?" she asked again.

"I hear them tell me ... I hear them tell me ... I hear them tell me ... to ... to ..."

I couldn't get the words out. The more I tried to get the words out, the more embarrassed and scared I became. She continued to hold me.

"It's okay, baby," she said, comforting me. "You can tell me," she said reassuringly.

I found the courage to tell my mom what I had been hearing. "I hear the voices telling me to kill myself."

It got quiet again. I lay in my mom's arms wondering how she would respond. My mom interrupted the silence and asked, "Have you just started hearing them, or have you heard them for a long time?"

"I just started hearing them." By this time, I was a little more comfortable. I sat up from leaning over the armrest and into my mom's side with her arm around me. I wiped my runny nose with the sleeve of my coat.

"Did something happen recently that you want to tell me about, or did the voices just start suddenly?"

"No, it just started." I was being honest. Nothing that I could think of had just happened to make me hear voices telling me to kill myself.

My mom said, "Baby, whenever you feel this way or whenever you hear these voices, I need you to tell me, okay?"

I nodded to show that I understood.

"Okay?" my mom asked again with a bit more force. My nod wasn't sufficient. She wanted a verbal answer.

"Okay," I said.

"Baby, don't give in to those thoughts or voices. Remember the scripture: 'Greater is He that is in you than he that is in the world.' Sometimes, it's not even you. The enemy can speak to us too, but you don't have to listen. You have God living in you. You understand?"

"Yes." I started to feel a great sense of peace as she spoke.

Some of my earliest memories involve my mom teaching me scriptures and explaining them to me.

"So the next time you hear something telling you to hurt yourself, you tell it, 'No! Greater is He that lives in me than he who is in the world!' And I want you to come to tell me. Okay?"

"Okay."

"Well, let me hear you say it. Greater is He that lives in me than he that lives in the world."

I repeated it softly. "Greater is He that lives in me than he that lives in the world."

"No." She corrected me. "Say it again like you know that you know that Jesus in you is greater."

I repeated it again, but this time, with more confidence.

"Say it again!"

I said it again, almost screaming it. I started smiling.

My mom smiled too. She grabbed my hand and prayed with me. We both said amen and drove home.

I never heard those voices again. Prayer works.

Kind Reminder
Tell Your Story

Sometimes, the person who needs to hear your story is you.

Laundry Day

IT WAS A sunny Saturday morning. I hadn't started my chores because I was watching cartoons: *Beekman's World*, *Teenage Mutant Ninja Turtles*, and *Garfield*. My mom was in the next room preparing to wash our clothes. During this time in my family's life, we struggled financially. We couldn't afford to purchase a dryer, but my mom and dad did manage to get us a washing machine that we purchased cheaply from the Scratch and Dent, a local place where you could get cheap appliances that were nicked, scratched, or otherwise less than perfect.

We didn't have any space for the washing machine in our small Philadelphia duplex, so we stored the washing machine next to the stove in our kitchen. It was an odd arrangement, but it worked for us. Plus, we didn't have many guests. When it was time to wash clothes, we would drag the machine next to the kitchen sink. If my dad was home, he would drag it to the sink for us. When he wasn't home, my mom and I would slide, wiggle, and pivot the machine to the sink the best way we could. One hose was connected to the sink faucet and held in place by a white rope, and the other larger hose was placed in the sink so the washing machine could get rid of unwanted water. During the spin cycle, the washing machine would jig and dance around on the kitchen floor. When the clothes were washed, we would hang them wherever there was space so they could dry: over the shower curtain bar, on the backs of doors, and sometimes even in the living room on the back of a chair. On laundry day, our small apartment would be filled with the scent of off-brand laundry detergent.

This Saturday, however, was a bit different. While my mom was washing clothes, we had run out of laundry detergent, and we didn't have any money to buy more. When you struggle financially, you become creative and sometimes desperate. To make do, mom used dishwashing liquid instead. A decision we soon learned was a big mistake. After loading the clothes into the washing machine, my mom went to her room to prepare the next load while I sat in the living room still glued to the television.

Beekman was teaching us how to make our own paper. "All you need is white glue, water, and some paper scraps!"

The washing machine was doing its usual jig across the kitchen floor when it suddenly began to gush out suds and soapy water as if the dish soap had given it such an upset stomach that it vomited.

I yelled to my mom. She whirled out of her room to see the floor covered in a quickly growing puddle of suds and soapy water. We tried to soothe the washing machine and get it to calm down. We turned off the water and turned all the knobs, but the sudsy vomiting continued, and the puddle of soapy water grew larger. Finally, my mom unplugged it. The washing machine, finally satiated, stopped its jigging and spewing.

A sigh of relief. I thought it was a moment of triumph and great victory. To me, a kid who still loved Power Rangers and Ninja Turtles, we had just saved the city and all of its inhabitants from the evil washing machine that spewed toxic, soapy water. We were heroes!

My mom, however, didn't share the same enthusiasm. She looked at all the suds on the floor, her soaked-through slippers, and the massive puddle of water she was standing in, and she wept. I couldn't figure out what was wrong or why she was crying. I tried to make it better by telling her everything would be alright. We had just fixed the problem with the washing machine and got it to stop dumping water on the floor. As my mom stood there, I finally realized that we weren't Power Rangers and that we didn't save the city by defeating an evil washing machine. This was reality. To her, *one more* thing had gone wrong, *one more* issue needed to be fixed, *one more* responsibility needed management, *one more* problem required a solution. She saw *one more* thing to carry on a back that was already overloaded.

Sometimes, *one more* can overwhelm even the strongest people.

The Grumblewog

WHEN I WAS growing up, my dad found ways to make me laugh, usually by acting like a big kid himself.

One evening, while it was dark outside, I was sitting on the edge of my bed in my bedroom, bored. My math textbook was resting on the bed next to me, and my notebook was on my lap. "I hate math," I whispered to myself.

Suddenly, the lights turned off, and the door to my bedroom slammed shut with a loud bang. I couldn't see anything. Everything was black.

"Mom? Dad?" I called out. No one answered. My heart started racing. I was afraid. "What's going on?" I asked myself.

In the darkness, I heard a hideous sound bellow out, an animal roar. It was loud and terrifying. The roar was followed by a series of snorts, growls, and grunts. I realized it was my dad.

I burst into laughter and tried my best to hide from him, tripping over clothes and sneakers that I threw on the floor earlier that day. He would snort and roar louder and rummage through my room until he found me. My room was very small, so there wasn't any place to hide. The door to my bedroom was behind him so I couldn't escape. I tried to hide in a corner. No matter where I tried to hide, he would always find me. When I was found, he would tickle me until I screamed in laughter and tears fell down my face.

The dreaded Grumblewog strikes again.

God Doesn't Draw Circles

USUALLY, AFTER SCHOOL, I would go to Ms. Tonya's house. My mom and dad would get home after I got out of school. They didn't feel I was responsible enough to have my own key or to stay home by myself, so Ms. Tonya watched me until they got home. Ms. Tonya was well known in the neighborhood and watched everyone's kids. She lived in a pretty house in the middle of my street. Her porch was always clean, and she never had trash near her steps. After school, all the kids would walk from school and go to Ms. Tonya's house. When we got there, we would all head down into the basement until our parents picked us up. It was a finished basement, but she didn't do much decorating down there. It had a small bathroom, a table and chairs for us to do our homework on, two sofas on either side of the walls, and one black and white television.

One day, while we were all playing in Ms. Tonya's basement, I started telling the other kids about Jesus.

I don't remember how the conversation started, but nonetheless, we were there. I told them that Jesus was real, that He loved us, and that God sent Him to die on the cross for our sins. I was surprised. I was only twelve years old, and the other kids were actually listening.

While I was sharing, however, one of the kids, Lilly, stood up and said, "I don't believe in God." She was about eleven years old and pretty, with long eyelashes and a great big mouth. "If God is real, tell Him to draw me a circle!" she said as she pointed to a nearby piece of paper and number two pencil with its eraser missing. I paused. I didn't know how to defend God.

"Lilly, it doesn't work like that. God doesn't have to prove anything."

Unmoved, she stared at the ceiling and yelled repeatedly, "Draw me a circle! Draw me a circle, God!"

We all got quiet to see what would happen. Without expressing it to each other, we all wanted to see if a glowing hand would appear, grab the pencil, and draw a circle. But nothing happened. God didn't move. God didn't respond. God didn't draw a circle.

Lilly broke the silence: "See, I told ya God wasn't real." Confident that she had proven the nonexistence of God, she walked away and went upstairs.

When she disappeared, I could feel the kids' eyes staring at me, watching to see what I would do. I was nervous because I didn't know whether my attempt to tell the kids about God's love was thwarted because God didn't draw a circle. I was tempted to change the subject and talk about school or something else. Instead, a boldness arose in me, and I continued to tell them about God. When I had finished, I asked them if they wanted to pray together. Another astonishing thing happened. They all agreed to pray together.

I asked them to hold hands and told them that I would lead them in prayer. Before I closed my eyes to lead the prayer, I looked around the circle in wonder because eight kids from ages nine to twelve were about to pray. I thought they would have been discouraged because of what happened between Lily and me moments ago, but they weren't. They still wanted to pray. After we prayed, there was a calm in Ms. Tonya's basement. The rest of our time together was spent laughing and talking.

Of all the remarkable moments in my life, this was one of the greatest.

The Dutiful Barber

MY FAMILY COULDN'T afford to get me haircuts like the other kids who had parts, fades, tight outlines, and designs. Instead, my dad cut my hair. I hated when my dad cut my hair. It's funny now, but back then, my dad cutting my hair was the demise of any chance I had at being popular. Lopsided fades, crooked parts, and uneven outlines were my dad's specialty.

Every other week, my dad would cut my hair, normally in the evening. We had a tall wooden chair with a faded, maroon leather seat. I would sit in the chair, legs swinging, praying and hoping that this time my haircut would be even. My dad didn't have all the tools and equipment that most barbers had, but he was a very resourceful man. He couldn't afford a barber's cape or expensive barber clippers. Instead, he used a thirteen-gallon trash bag and tied it around my neck. My neck would sweat and itch through the entire haircut. My scalp was at the mercy of my dad and his clippers. My scalp was a humble sacrifice, my dad was the priest, and the cheap clippers were the sacrificial blade.

He then would spend what seemed like hours cleaning the clippers and trying to set the blades. Whenever I got haircuts, despite the inevitable disaster and impending doom soon to be my haircut, the buzzing of the blades across my scalp relaxed me until *bizzzzzz*. My dad had fallen asleep again and nicked me.

When he had finished cutting my hair, proud of his latest creation, he would tell me to look in the mirror in the bathroom, which was right behind the kitchen in our small two-bedroom duplex.

"Dad, it's crooked!" I'd yell from the bathroom.

"No, it's not. That's just the cut hair that hasn't fallen off yet. When you wash your hair, it will be even," he would shoot back.

Washing my hair never made my haircut even.

My Buddy Quinton

IT WAS A weekday, and I was getting ready for school. While I was going about my morning routine, the phone rang. It was pretty early for the phone to ring. My grandmother always taught me to never call anyone before 10:30 a.m. I shrugged it off and started laying out my clothes to get ironed as I hummed a random song.

My mom answered. I didn't hear what she was saying.

She called me into the living room to join her and my dad, who was sitting on the sofa. I came walking in with a huge smile.

"Yes, mom!"

"Honey, sit down. I have to tell you something." She patted on the sofa in a space between her and my dad, showing me where she wanted me to sit. Something was wrong. When I sat down, she grabbed my hand.

"Okay, what's wrong?"

"I'm so sorry, honey."

I looked over at my dad. I could see the sadness in his eyes. I'd seen my dad upset before, but I never saw him sad.

"Sorry about what, Mom?"

"Do you have a friend named Quinton?"

"Yeah, he lives down the street. We both draw, and he comes to Ms. Tonya's house so she can watch him sometimes."

"Honey, I have some bad news." She took a deep breath. "Quinton got into a car accident yesterday, and he …"

She took another deep breath and exhaled sharply. "He didn't survive it, baby. I'm so, so, so sorry."

I was numb. This was my first experience with death, and I didn't know how to respond to it. In my heart, I felt a deep sadness for which there were no words; my stomach felt as if it had detached from my body and was flipped inside out, while a million thoughts were running through my head trying to make sense of the news I had just heard. Growing up on Fifteenth Street, I only had three friends. Quinton was one of them. We were around the same age, and we shared many of the same interests.

My head dropped. I started to sniffle. My mom put her arms around me and held me. "It's okay, sweetie. We got you." I started to cry.

"I'm so sorry, honey. I'm so, so, so, so sorry, honey. We're here."

My dad's big arms wrapped around my mom and me. "It's okay, son. We got you. It's okay, son."

Tyrone

Y MOM, DAD, and I were waiting at the Olney Transportation Center for the C bus to arrive so we could go to church. It was one of those cold and sunny Sunday mornings where the sun shined proudly, the sky was light and blue, and the air was cold and crisp with random whips of wind. I felt the cold air on my neck as it found its way through the gaps in my loosely wrapped scarf. I didn't care. It actually felt pretty good. Buses still groggy from last night's late commutes moaned and growled as they picked up and dropped off passengers at their stops. Usually, there aren't many people at the transportation center on a Sunday this early. They're probably still asleep.

Newspapers, empty beer and soda cans, candy wrappers, and dry leaves spun and rolled on the floor of the transportation as they were pulled and dragged by the wind. I watched as they moved about as if they were moving on their own. It was still a beautiful and peaceful morning. Even with the trash. While I was enjoying the cold sun air, I saw a man across the street walking toward the side of the street where we were standing.

It was Tyrone! I'm not sure if that was his name, but it's the name I gave him. I'm not sure why I gave him that name. I didn't see Tyrone often. Sometimes I would see him a day or two during the week when I caught the bus home from school and sometimes on Sunday mornings when my family and I caught the bus to head to church.

A herd of pigeons plucking at a small piece of pretzel seemed unbothered as he walked closer to them but eventually moved as he walked by them still plucking at the piece of pretzel.

Tyrone's walk was slow. He slid his feet when he walked but seemed to walk on his tippy-toes at the same time. He was a little shorter than my dad, who is about six feet tall, and he was thin and lanky. His hair was salt and pepper colored. Coils of it peeked from beneath his black Scully. He had a full beard, which was also salted and peppered, but more salt than pepper, and was coarse and unruly. He wore two or three pairs of pants, maybe three or four shirts, and an unbuttoned black wool trench coat that hung on him because it was too big.

Tyrone made his way to one of the trash cans, leaned over it, and slowly started moving the trash around from side to side. The few people who were at the transportation center who saw him looked in disgust. Some who were standing close to where he was moved. Tyrone didn't care. He seemed not to notice them. He was looking for something. A whip of wind made the tails of his coat dance. He moved to another trash can and dug through the trash again. This time he paused. He found what he was looking for. His arm disappeared as he reached deep into the mouth of the silver trash can. I looked on in curiosity, trying not to let him see I was watching him. He pulled out what he was looking for. A red French fry box. Tyrone was hungry and was looking for something to eat. He tilted the box and emptied the remaining fries into his mouth and threw the box back in the trash. Tyrone walked away and disappeared behind the corner.

One man's trash may be another man's meal. Be grateful.

Eggs, Bacon, and Insulin

MAYBE I WAS ready to wake up, or maybe it was the smell of crispy bacon popping and sizzling in the kitchen. In my usual foggy way, I sat on the edge of my bed and waited for the rest of the grogginess to wear off. I yawned wide, stretched, got up, put my slippers on, and swayed my limp body to the kitchen, allowing the wall to catch me. Through cracked eyes, I saw my mom standing at the stove with her robe tied loosely around her and wearing some blue slippers.

"Good morning, baby."

"Good morning, Mom."

"You sleep well?"

"Yes."

"Good."

"Breakfast is almost done."

My dad came into the kitchen shortly after I did.

Between us three, my dad was the morning person and always gave us a cheerful morning greeting.

"Hey, hon," he said. He and my mom kissed. "Tommie-o, good morning son."

"Hey, dad," I said.

By then I started to wake up. The smell of bacon, eggs, and French toast saturated the air. I watched as my mom flipped over another slice of white bread in the egg and cinnamon custard and then dropped it into the hot pan.

While my dad and I were talking, my mom turned off the stove, made our plates, and disappeared into the backroom to lay down.

I sat down with my plate and squeezed a bunch of syrup on the French toast. I barely chewed, shoving the French toast down. Before I could even swallow the last mouthful, my fork danced and whirled across the plate making syrup streaks as I gathered the next scoopful. My dad and I were catching up because I hadn't seen him that much that week because of his work schedule. He asked me about school, friends, and my week. While I was in mid-gorge and we were in mid-conversation, my dad got back up to start working on his second plate. As I ate, I could hear the spoon scraping the frying pan to scoop up more eggs, but then it grew oddly quiet. No conversation, no jokes, no scraping of the pan, nothing. I didn't think much of it, so I kept eating.

Then *boom.*

The noise was so loud that my heart almost leaped out of my chest. I turned quickly and looked at the stove and didn't see my dad. I lowered my eyes, and I saw him on the ground. He was shivering, twitching, and convulsing with foam coming out of the side of his mouth. I could only see the whites of his eyes because they were rolled in the back of his head. I didn't know what to say or how to respond. I had never seen this before. I rushed out of my chair and kneeled next to him and called him repeatedly.

"Dad! Dad!" I called. He continued to tremble.

"Dad! Wake up. Please!" I said tapping his shoulder. He continued to shake.

He wouldn't respond, so I screamed as loud as I could for my mom. "Mom! Mom! Mom!" She rushed into the room with the belt of her robe trailing behind her, yelling the whole way.

"What? What? What is it? What's wrong?"

"It's Dad!"

When she got into the kitchen and saw him lying on the floor she screamed. "Oh, Lord! Honey." She knelt down next to him and tapped him repeatedly on his shoulder. "Can you hear me? Talk to me. Honey, talk to me, please."

"Tommie, call 911! Tell them where we live, open the door, and stand outside so they know where to go!" I shot up from the floor and grabbed the house phone and called 911. After I got off the phone with them, I did as my mom instructed and opened the door and stood on the porch so the ambulance would know where to go. I stood outside on the porch looking up and down the block to see which end the ambulance would be coming from. Anxiety and fear were building up inside of me.

It was odd. Despite the panic my family and I were feeling, the neighborhood was oddly peaceful. The birds were still singing, no cars were driving, and everyone was still in their homes as if the emergency in my home wasn't happening. The peace in the neighborhood was interrupted by the faint sound of sirens. The ambulance was on its way. As the sound grew louder, my fear and worry started to subside because help was on the way.

When the ambulance finally got there, my dad had started coming around. He was confused and couldn't remember anything that had happened. He is a diabetic, and something happened with his insulin levels. The EMTs placed my dad in the back of the ambulance to take him to the hospital to ensure he was okay. That was one of the scariest moments of my life.

The Tumbling Bag

IT CAUGHT MY eye while I was staring out the window. The somersaulting, flipping, turning, twisting, and tumbling high in the sky on invisible balance beams with agility, grace, and delight. It was a welcome distraction from the humdrum routine of another day of school.

A white plastic bag that had "Thank You" written on it. Soaring freely, high in the air, unnoticed by the people walking below and the cars driving lazily on the street. The leaves on the street corners and in the gutters rustle and spin, aroused by the gentle gusts of wind. But their dance is rigid. Not free and fluid like the bag.

I stared, dazed, watching the bag, wishing I too were free like it. No worries. Just free to soar and flip in the wind.

"Mr. Suggs, are you with us?" my teacher yelled from the front of the room with her hands on her hips. I was caught in another daze. It was the third time this week.

This is your fault, bag.

Kind Reminder
Cuts and Wounds

THE BAD NEWS: Wounds can take a second to create and a lifetime to heal.
The good news: Healing is still possible.

Wednesday Nights

GROWING UP, WEDNESDAYS were the longest day of the week for my family and me, which made them tough. My mom worked during the day, and I went to school, but afterward, we both would head to Bible Study. Sometimes my dad would go with us, but usually, he had to work.

During this time in my family's life, we didn't own a car, so we took public transportation everywhere: buses, trains, and regional rail. Sundays and Wednesdays were the toughest because while we lived in Philadelphia, our church was in another part of Pennsylvania. It would only take forty-five minutes to drive there, but it seemed like a lifetime to get there by SEPTA.

From school, I had to catch the Eighth and Market train (or as I called it, "the train with the yellow lights"). The Eighth and Market train is what I caught to meet my mom at the Gallery. All the trains in Philly looked alike during this time. No matter where they were headed, they had a silver exterior with hard orange and beige seats. I'm sure the people who cleaned the trains did the best they could, but they always seemed dirty. Wet sunflower seeds in a seat, graffiti, foreign liquids creeping on the floor near your foot, and potato chip bags in between the seats. Sometimes when I was bored, when the train sped off, if there were two or more empty soda cans or bottles rolling around on the floor, I would watch to see which piece of trash moved the quickest.

Usually, the train stops smelled like urine and had trash scattered everywhere. Some stops smelled stronger than others, but most of them smelled like urine.

My mom worked downtown, which is where the Gallery was, at one of the offices doing administrative work. For work, she usually wore a blouse, skirt, and sneakers, carrying her work shoes in a shopping bag. After giving her a tight hug and kiss, we would speed to the food court to grab some pizza or Chinese food, then sit at one of the food court tables, and scarf down our meal so we don't miss our train, trying to talk over our mouthfuls of food to catch up on each other's day.

After we had finished eating, we would head to the ticket counter to purchase our tickets for the R6. "Now, Tommie, don't lose this ticket," she always told me. "If you do, you're staying here." We'd both laugh as we headed to the platform to board the train. The platform was usually filled with all types of people going here and there for whatever purpose or reason. Some going home, others heading to another job.

It didn't usually take long for the train to come and for me to see its two bold, glowing white eyes staring back at me from the dark tunnel as it screeched in the distance, moving closer to the platform. The train would pull up, and if you were lucky when the train stopped, you were standing in front of one of its doors. When we boarded the train, it was usually packed. We wouldn't get a seat until we got closer to our stop and passengers started getting off the train. My mom and I would stand next to one another, swaying on the silver poles as the train sped along.

Usually, folks in suits, dress suits, briefcases, roller bags, and newspapers rode this train. I always felt weird riding with them because they all seemed very important. Like they had great careers, were happy, and were financially stable. It never seemed like my mom and I belonged. They rode the train because they wanted to. We rode the train because we had to. Their clothes looked expensive. Ours were a combination of items given to us by close friends and family and items from Value City. Their shoes looked expensive and shiny. My sneakers were scuffed and dingy, and my mom had her shoes in a Shop Rite grocery bag we had used to carry onions, green peppers, and crackers. They looked content, peaceful, and happy. We looked as though we were just trying to make it through another week.

Reflection
Let Him Speak

I TRIED LOCKING HIM away and hiding him, but he would not have it. He refused to be silenced, and I couldn't ignore him any longer. The boy in me had something to say. I decided to let him speak. I'm ready for the conversation now.

Philly Mean Face

MY MOM AND I had been standing in the living room for almost thirty minutes. She was grilling me.

"Make a mean face," she demanded, getting frustrated after my many failed previous attempts at making a mean face.

I tightened my eyes and scowled as hard as I could, trying to keep myself from bursting into laughter.

"No, meaner," she commanded.

I tightened my eyes to where they almost closed and scowled so hard that my cheeks were starting to ache.

My mom was teaching me how to make what I call "the Philly Mean Face."

The Philly Mean Face is a face a lot of Philadelphians have. Sometimes, I think my fellow Philadelphians are born with it. It's a face that says a few things: "Try me if you want to," "I've had a bad day and I'm waiting for someone to say something so I can go off," and "I'm the wrong one to mess with."

Philly can be a tough place to live, and if you don't look like you're from around here or like you have a rough edge, you can easily become a target.

Adopting a mean face felt unnatural, but I had to adapt to the culture and environment around me to survive. I was a good kid who loved animals and people and always smiled. I was more concerned with saving the whales and the pollution in our ocean than showing I was tough. My mom always said, "Son, it's a dog-eat-dog world." Though I never really knew what that meant, I had an idea of what she was trying to say. She was preparing me for a reality and a world that couldn't care less about me or my whales.

"Okay, let's try again. And this time, show me your walk."

I tried again and made the meanest face I could. My brow sunk, and I frowned with the hardest frown I could muster. I slouched and strutted in front of my mom. I looked horrible.

"That's your mean face and your walk?" I could hear the disappointment in her voice.

I burst into laughter. "Oh mighty and powerful Philly Mean Face Master, please forgive me, your humble disciple, for not mastering the hidden art of Mean-Facing."

"You better stop laughing and learn how to make a mean face," she said, more seriously than I anticipated.

"It's a deterrent. These fools out here are crazy, and you need to be able to show them not to mess with you. Now show me again."

I could hear the concern and seriousness in her voice. I tried again. I squinted and made my lips and jaws tights.

"How's this?" I asked through my tight jaws, not moving my lips.

"What is that?"

"It's my mean face, see?"

My mom was split between laughing and being frustrated.

"Lord, help my son. Go finish your homework."

I think my Philly Mean Face is broken.

The Weather Woman

IT WAS MONDAY morning, and I had just woken up. I finally managed to sit upright in the bed with my feet dangling off the side of the bed. I put on my slippers and made my way to the kitchen where my mom was making breakfast. She had the news on. I never really paid attention to the news. It's usually depressing story after depressing story.

"Another fatal blaze in California. We wish the families who were caught in this tragedy well. Now, for the weather. Hope, tell us what we can expect today!"

I hate it when she gives the forecast because she's usually wrong.

"Sunny skies, with no chance of rain and a high in the midseventies. A perfect day for outdoor activities. Get outside and enjoy some of this beautiful weather. Jason, back to you!"

I walked to the window and pulled open the curtain.

It wasn't sunny. The weather wasn't beautiful, and it wasn't the perfect day for outdoor activities. It was cold. Rainy. Bitter. Brittle. Pearls of rain glided down the window until they reached the cracked white paint on the windowsill.

I hate when Hope lies.

Kind Reminder
Shoes and Laces

THEY SAY, "BEFORE you judge someone, walk a mile in their shoes." But walking in someone else's shoes is easy.

Lacing up and walking in your own is what's hard.

Poppa Has a Secret

I T WAS HAPPENING again.

He quivered and shook as faint whines and mumblings escaped his lips. Tormenting visions and memories flashed and darted across his mind. Each one was worse than the last. Small beads of sweat formed on his distorted brow.

The strength he proudly touted was beginning to fail him. His strong arms and back trembled, buckled beneath the weight of the secrets he carried for years. No one told Poppa that secrets were heavy.

His breathing intensified; his veins bulged, his sweat now pouring.

Between all the mumbling and whining, the only words that could be understood were "no" and "please." The memories and stories that he repressed during the day were unrelenting and haunted him in the evening. He was drowning in himself. When he was a child, his young eyes saw too much, and he was told what happened in this house stayed in this house. He was taught not to speak. It's not that Poppa didn't care. He'd been muted his entire life and was never given permission to speak. He was told that men don't cry, so Poppa stopped crying a long time ago. Never taught that he should share his story, he did the only thing he knew to do. He swallowed it. He swallowed his stories and his trauma, devouring each page, every word, period, and sentence. Often sickened by the pungent aftertaste of his own ink. The stories, abuse, and aguish rolled around in his belly until he vomited up everything. Each page, sentence, and period. He vomited in silence and alone. Wiping off the question marks that dripped from his chin with his sleeve so he could continue to give the appearance of strength.

Black men are not just traumatized because of what happens to them. They are traumatized because they are never given permission to talk about it. Silence is traumatizing.

The stories he tried to run away from found him.

"No!" he commanded. "No!" he said again. But this time, he was begging as if whatever it was had overpowered him. He was trying to stop it from happening.

"No!" Poppa sat up and gasped for air.

Poppa was dreaming.

Author's Note: This story is not about my dad as I have never witnessed him having a traumatic dream. I did, however, feel it was important to touch on trauma among black men and how there are few places and people that give men permission to process it.

Reflection
Misplaced Tear Ducts

ALL MEN CRY. But not all tears are made of water.

Kind Reminder
Polished Armor

WE SPEND so much time polishing our armor that we forget to tend to the warrior hemorrhaging beneath it. The appearance of strength is overrated. Your warrior needs you.

Lawns and Mowers

"**Y**OU EVER USE one of these, boy?" he asked sharply with his heavy country accent.

"No," I said, looking at the pile of metal with four black wheels.

"No? You ain't mowing the lawn in Philly?" he said. I could hear the judgment in his voice.

"We don't have lawns in Philly," I responded.

I was about fourteen years old and was visiting my uncle and aunt down south during the summer as I did most summers. I was on punishment for staying out too late with some friends I had just made. Cell phones were not popular back then. If you were out, you would have to wait until you got to a payphone or someone's house to use their landline to make a call. My curfew was 9:00 p.m., but I came in at almost 10:00 p.m. after walking around the neighborhood with my new friends. My uncle and aunt didn't know where I was, and they were worried, so mowing the lawn was my punishment for making them worry and breaking my curfew.

Visiting with my uncle and aunt was always an occasion of culture shock. Boys down south were given more freedom, had more responsibilities, and were expected to function as men. There were boys who were younger than me who knew how to cook breakfast and mow lawns. Boys up north didn't have much responsibility. I could tell by my uncle's questions and tone that he didn't think much of how boys up north were groomed.

"What are they teaching you boys up there?" he asked in disappointment as we stood facing each other separated by the lawnmower. "Okay, well, first, you need to start the mower. I just filled it up, so it should have enough gas. Yank this cord to start it. Keep yanking until it starts. Keep your hands and feet away from the blades and push it forward. You got that?"

"Yes, I got it."

I yanked the cord; the mower sputtered in annoyance. I yanked it again; this time the mower scoffed defiantly. It still wouldn't start. Like with a rebellious horse that refused to be ridden, I had not earned the mower's respect.

"Give it here, boy." My uncle, frustrated with my city-boy attempts to start the mower, grabbed it and yanked the cord hard, one time. The mower sprung to life and started to purr loudly as if the mower was waiting for my uncle's golden touch.

"Now, push this up and down the lawn. I'll be in

the house." And with that, it was just me and the angry lawnmower.

I started pushing the mower up and down the lawn. I was at it for almost thirty minutes, heaving and grunting behind a mower that didn't want to move and seemed to be pushing back. Beads of sweat piled on my head and rolled down the back of my neck and face. I was in mid complaint when my uncle broke my concentration. He had come back outside to check on my progress. "Boy! What the heck are you doing?!" he screamed from the porch before walking toward me quickly.

"Look at what you did to my lawn. I said, 'up and down.' You went zig zag. They don't teach y'all how to mow lawns?" he yelled. I recalled him asking me this same question before I started mowing. My answer was no then, and it was no now. Instead of responding or sharing my sarcastic thoughts, which would surely have gotten me in trouble, I decided not to respond.

I guess the flower patch wasn't supposed to be mowed.

"That's enough. Give it here. I'll do it. Go in the house and clean up. Your aunt just made us some lunch."

Usually, I enjoyed my time down south, but this time wasn't too enjoyable.

I hate lawnmowers and lawns.

Red Balloon

ITS RED, PLUMP, glossy skin shined, sparkled in the sun. As I stood and watched in anticipation, my eyes widened, my heart raced, and I smiled. After a short while, it finally came close enough for me to grab. My red balloon. Full and plump like a harvest moon and almost juicy like a sweet plum.

The white string dangled lazily, inviting me to grab it. It was here to carry me away. It always knew when to come. As if it could sense my need for it.

I grabbed the white string tightly, and the balloon lifted me off the ground. My feet gradually lifted from the ground as my tippy-toes scraped the gray sidewalk.

"Another pair of sneakers scuffed up. My mom is going to kill me."

The balloon floated higher and higher until my feet no longer touched the ground.

I floated until there were no more car horns, yellow streetlights, gunshots, hurt, rejection, or pigeons.

Kind Reminder
Time

TIME IS NOT a physician. It cannot heal all wounds.

The Putt Putt

IT HAD BEEN a few months, but my mom and dad finally got a car. It was the end of waiting on cold corners for the bus, long train rides, and sharing space with a bunch of strangers. They purchased it from a used car lot with money they had been saving. It was an older car. It was a small, light-blue, four-door car. For the first month or two, it ran well, but shortly thereafter, we started having problems with it. Two of the biggest problems were that the rear passenger-side window fell out and that the car started smoking horribly every time it started. The missing window wasn't a huge issue for me. We replaced it with a piece of cardboard or a trash bag. When it rained, I would just sit on the driver's side of the car next to the side that had a window. Problem solved. The smoke, however, was an entirely different issue because it was extremely embarrassing. It seemed to smoke the most on Sunday mornings. At least to me, it did. After we left the house to pack into the car, I would immediately slide down so none of the neighbors could see my face. I was preparing for the embarrassing moment getting ready to take place. My dad put the key into the ignition and turned the car on. Without fail, the exhaust would spew so much smoke that it almost covered the entire neighborhood in a white sheet of smoke. My mom and dad, who were unbothered by the thick midst created by the four-wheeled fog machine, would take their time, drink their coffee, and finish their conversation that started in the house. The entire time, I would be begging my dad to pull off under my breath. "Leave. Leave. Leave. Please just leave, Dad." I would sink lower into the back seat. My mom and dad would continue to engage in casual conversation, unaware of the meltdown happening behind them. Eventually, after the car had warmed up and they had destroyed enough of the ozone layer, my dad would put the car in gear, and we would head to church.

Of course, leaving a trail of smoke behind us.

Coins For a Cut

ONE DAY, AFTER school, I told my dad that I wanted to get a haircut from an actual barber instead of letting him cut my hair. Money was tight, and my family just couldn't afford for me to get a haircut. I guess I begged long enough because my dad finally gave in. He promised he would take me the following week after school.

I got home, and we drove to a barber that he knew well in West Philadelphia. The neighborhood where the barbershop was located seemed a little rough. It had a few vacant homes with boarded windows, sneakers dangled from the powerline, and someone arguing up the street. When we walked in, we were greeted warmly by the barber. I could tell that he and my dad knew each other well and had been close friends for a long time. We didn't make an appointment, and the barber had a few people in front of me, so we had to wait for the next available opening. Seeing sharp cut after sharp cut made me even more eager to get my own. The barber had pinpoint precision. Sharp outlines, double points, fades, fros, waves, and beards. I wanted it all.

Soon, it was my turn to sit in the smooth, black leather chair trimmed with silver. I sat down; the seat was still warm from the previous client. The barber snapped the black barber's cape with the shop's white initials in the air to get rid of the excess hair and fastened it around my neck.

"So what you get'n, lil man?"

"Can you bring it down some and make it even all around with points and a fade on the neck?"

"I gotchu."

"What grade you in, lil man?" he asked while he brushed my hair and tilted my head for the perfect angle.

"Seventh," I said quickly, trying to contain my nervousness and excitement. He spun me around. When the chair stopped, he tilted my head to the right. I quickly glanced around the perimeter of the room. My dad was sitting against the wall with the other five customers. I could tell he was tired. His eyes were growing heavy, and his head was starting to bob as he tried to keep himself awake. Rap music played in the background.

Having a real barber's cape wrapped around my neck instead of the plastic kitchen trash bag that my dad used felt good. The clippers felt good too. I could tell he used the good clippers because they buzzed differently. His clippers had a deep, smooth buzz sound, while my dad's clippers were loud, high pitched, annoying, and always nicked me. Soon, he was done. He brushed the excess hair off my face, wiped my edges down with a piece of tissue he soaked quickly in alcohol, and handed me the mirror. I struggled to grab it because the cape was covering my hands. I turned from side to side in disbelief. It was better than I had imagined. A low cut with double points and a fade on the neck like I asked. Perfect!

I handed him back the mirror. He took the cape off, snapped it in the air again to remove the hair for the next client, and told my dad how much the cut costs.

"A'ight man, that will be ten dollas."

While I stood there between them both, proud of my new haircut, my dad reached in his pocket and fumbled around a bit. Eventually, his hand reappeared from his pocket in the form of a tight fist. When he opened his hand, it was filled with a bunch of loose change. Quarters, nickels, dimes, and a penny. My dad took his index finger and started to slide the coins around in his massive palm to divide the coins into dollars. My dad was going to pay the barber in coins. At that moment, my family's financial hardship became vividly clear to me. As a kid, you don't really pay attention to the bills, the cost of food, or utilities. Food was always on the table. The lights were always on. I may not have had the clothes I wanted, but I still had clothes to wear. Though my family's financial hardship became clear, I was still a little embarrassed by the handful of quarters, nickels, and dimes. I wanted my dad to pay with a ten- or twenty-dollar bill like the other kids' dads. I dropped my eyes to the ground so I wouldn't notice if anyone saw us.

The barber smiled and kindly declined and said the haircut was on the house. My dad stuffed the coins back into his pocket. They both smiled, shook hands, and we left to head home.

As a kid, I thought that was an embarrassing moment, but as an adult, I see that as one of the kindest, purest, sweetest, and most sacrificial actions. Though my dad didn't have much, he was willing to give all he had. Even if it was just coins.

Saltpeppaketchup

"SHRIMP FRIED RICE, four wings with salt-pep-pa-ketchup, one egg roll with extra duck sauce, and a Pepsi."

In Philly, "saltpeppaketchup" goes on everything.

Yes, it's one word.

Kind Reminder
Self-Kindness

B E KIND TO you, even when you feel you are unworthy of your own kindness. Forgive you. Love you. You deserve you. All of you.

Momma,
Wednesday, and Grits

THE SKY HADN'T opened her eyes, and the sun was still deep in her slumber. Quiet was in the air, and a holy hush filled the room. It was Wednesday morning.

Early morning. No noise, no sun, just momma, her grits, and her thoughts. The unbroken quiet was only interrupted by the occasional sliding of momma's feet on the kitchen vinyl floor and the sound of grits being stirred in the pot. She always uses the same pot when she makes them. Momma rose early as she did every morning to take care of us. Hair still in rollers, dressed in a nightgown, with an old robe wrapped snugly around her.

My dad and I were still fast asleep.

She scraped the sides of the plastic container of butter to scoop the last bit of butter. It was freckled with toast crumbs; it was just enough. Payday day wasn't until Friday. She made the last eggs we had left.

Momma stirred the grits, and the combination of momma's tired morning eyes and the gentle sound of the wooden spoon scraping the sides and bottom of the pot took her mind elsewhere.

Lord, I'm tired. Ike is working a double shift tonight, so I need to pack extra lunch for him. I feel bad because he's been working so hard and has been so tired lately, but we really need the money. So many of our bills are past due. I don't know how we're gonna make it. Lord, please make a way.

Tommie needs new sneakers and new dress pants. He's growing so fast. My baby.

She said to herself proudly. Momma chuckled to herself and shook her head with a grin.

I need to help Nana get to her appointment. I gotta remember to tell my boss I need off on the twenty-seventh. Goodness, my boss and his assistant, Rebecca. Mmm, mmm, mmm. The blind lead'n the blind. At least he's nice.

That Rebecca on the other hand ... goodness. She's as mean as the day is long. I gotta finish that work she threw on my desk at the end of the day yesterday. I'll let God take care of her. Always with her nose in the air. She wouldn't be so arrogant if she knew she always had that cheap lipstick on her teeth. Lord, forgive me.

I don't know what we're going to do about this electric bill. I'm surprised the lights are still on. God is good. I'll try to get an extension on the water bill and use the money we were going to use for the water bill and put it toward the electric bill to at least hold them off.

Maybe I can borrow some money from Tammy. Just enough for lunch meat, cheese, eggs, butter, and … and … laundry detergent. That's it. I need to wash these stockings, and Tommie's shirts are starting to smell. It's Wednesday now, and payday ain't until next Friday.

You can do it, girl. Just a few more days. You got this.

Momma took a deep breath and then released it.

The grits bubbled and steamed. Momma turned the pot off and added slices of cheese, salt, and pepper, stirring it until the mix is well blended and creamy. Eggs and bacon sizzled in the frying pan next to the grits. She heard my dad shuffle to the shower.

A mouse squeaked in the corner. She didn't bother to turn to see. Momma wasn't afraid of mice, and it was too early for the hunt. Roaches, on the other hand, she couldn't stand those.

It's another Wednesday morning, another pot of grits, and momma with her thoughts.

Lie Detector

"**H**EY, HOW DO you think lie detectors work?" Sam asked one day while we were walking home from school. Sam and I lived in the same neighborhood and attended the same middle school.

"You mean them things that can tell if you lyin' or tell'n the truth?" I asked.

"Yeah …"

"They read your mind, duh." I was very confident in my answer.

"Well, my dad told me that lie detectors read your heart rate, and that's how they tell if you're lyin'."

"Heart rate?! What's a heart rate gotta do with telling if somebody is lyin'? The machine reads your mind. Your dad is dumb."

"Don't call my dad dumb. Your dad is dumb and so is your mom. My dad is a police officer and knows all about that stuff."

"Well, your dad should know that lie detectors read your mind. So your dad is still dumb."

We walked the rest of the way home debating how lie detectors work. We ended our debate at the end of the driveway. He lived the next block over and used the driveway as a shortcut to get home.

Later in life, I found out that lie detectors don't read your mind.

He was right.

His dad is still dumb.

Waves

"**M**om … Mom … Mom! Hurry!" I yelled from the bathroom of our small two-bedroom duplex. I was wearing a wrinkled white T-shirt, black sweatpants, and old white socks, and I had just removed a stocking I stole from my mom's drawer that I was using as a wave cap from my head.

My mom came running into the bathroom with the usual wrinkle on her brow that appeared whenever she was concerned, worried, or angry. I could tell the wrinkle in her brow this time was because of concern or worry.

"What's wrong, baby?" I could hear the concern and worry in her voice.

"They're coming in!" I told her.

Confused, my mom asked, "What's coming in?" The wrinkle in her brow got deeper.

"My waves! See, see, see!"

I held my head closer to the light that rested above the mirror so she could see the fruits of my labor. Months of brushing, wearing my mom's stockings on my head so tight they gave me headaches, and smearing pomade on my scalp was starting to pay off. Three faint ripples.

"That's nice, baby. That's really nice," she said as she looked closely at my hair to inspect my waves. Her face and voice softened, and the wrinkle in her brow disappeared.

I smiled ear to ear.

Getting waves had become all that I could think about. All the boys in my school either had waves or were trying hard to get them. Though I couldn't afford name-brand clothes and didn't fit in, I was on my way. Three faint ripples were a great starting place.

Flesh Wound

H E RELOADED HIS weapon quickly and easily, using his fingers to feel the cold skin of each bullet as he directed them into the chamber, never taking his eye off his target. The day before he missed, but this time, he was determined to hit his mark. An experienced marksman. After he reloaded, he inhaled through his nostrils and then exhaled slowly, emptying his lungs, allowing the warm air to pass over his dry, cracked lips. He steadied himself, controlled his breathing, aimed, and waited.

Without warning or permission, he fired. The sound of the blast echoed as one bullet was released from his chamber: a word.

"B*TCH!" It was hot, searing, and painful. The word tore through my confidence, almost piercing my heart. The words that pierce the heart are the worst. They're hard to heal from and can sometimes be fatal. Words are powerful. Luckily, this was only a flesh wound. I'll live.

Reflection
Mirror Mirror

Mirror mirror on the wall ...

...

...

...

...

Never mind ...

Same Name

THE BEIGE CORDED phone with the coil cord blared from across the room where I had been watching television, demanding an answer.

I ran to the phone to answer it, hoping to quickly end the conversation with whoever was on the other end so I could go back to watch television.

"Hello," I said quickly, trying to move the conversation along.

"Hello. May I please speak to Tommie Suggs?" It was a man whose voice I wasn't familiar with. He didn't sound like anyone in my family or any of my parent's friends. Plus, he had an accent like my family who lives down south in Charlotte. Still unsure of who the caller was and why he was looking for me, I reluctantly obliged.

"This is he. May I ask who this is?" Very early in my upbringing, my mother and grandmother taught me how to answer the phone. I was practicing my skills on this unknown caller.

"Yeah. It's Tommie Suggs," he responded. The line got quiet for a few seconds while I tried to figure out why he gave me my name when I asked for his.

"What? No, what's your name?" I asked him again, overenunciating my words in case he didn't hear me the first time.

"Tommie Suggs." He gave me the same answer. At this point, I was confused and started to become annoyed.

"No, *my* name is Tommie Suggs," I argued.

"My name is Tommie Suggs too." I could hear the lightheartedness in his voice. I didn't know what was going on, and I started to feel uncomfortable talking to a stranger.

I didn't know what else to say so I hung up the phone. A few minutes later, the phone rang again.

"Hello. May I speak to Tommie Suggs?" the caller asked again. I could hear a tinge of frustration in his voice because I hung up on him.

"Who is this?" I asked, hoping to get his real name and reason for calling.

"My name is Tommie Suggs."

"Sir, stop calling."

I hung up the phone again.

My mom appeared out of the backroom with a confused and annoyed look on her face.

"Who keeps calling here?" she asked. I could hear the irritation in her voice.

"Some man who keeps asking for me. When I ask him what his name is, he keeps saying his name is Tommie, but that's my name so I hung up on him."

My mom's look of confusion deepened while she tried to piece everything together. Suddenly, my mom's face softened, and the wrinkle in her forehead disappeared.

"Baby, when the phone rings again, I'll answer it. I think I know what's going on."

The next time the phone rang, my mom answered it. I knew it was the same person even though I couldn't hear their voice.

"Oh heeey. Wow. How have you been? Mmhmm. Mmhmm. Mmhmm." She responded after each thing the caller said. "Well, it's good to hear from you. I'll put him on."

My mom buried the phone in her chest so the caller couldn't hear what she was saying.

"The phone is for you. It's your father. Your biological father."

My mom and my biological dad met in Atlanta, GA, while they were both serving in the army. While I was still a baby, my mom and my biological father went their separate ways. He stayed in Atlanta, and my mom and I moved to Philadelphia, PA, to stay with my grandmother in the West Oak Lane part of the city. When I was about ten years old, my mom met and married my stepfather (my dad through marriage).

After this moment, my biological dad forever became a part of my life and is one of my favorite people.

I have two dads. One dad through birth and the other through marriage. I appreciate them both, cherish them both, and love them both immensely.

Kind Reminder
Bumper Sticker

TODAY I SAW a bumper sticker that said,
"STUDENT DRIVER."
Aren't we all?

Mom, Do You Love Me?

I T WAS THE end of another school day, and I was happy to be home. The day turned quickly to night because it was during the winter when it gets dark early. The streetlights were already on. I could see them peeking into the apartment between the closed cream blinds.

I had already kicked off my sneakers and was sitting on the tan floral print sofa in the living room of our small duplex, working on math problems. I hated seventh-grade math. I could never get the right answers. My marble notebook was on my lap, and the math textbook was resting next to me. A rogue pencil rolled away and hid between the sofa cushions, hoping I wouldn't find it so I couldn't dull its pointed head with my hard writing.

My mom had been home for about an hour, so she had already changed out of her work clothes into a navy-blue T-shirt with white writing, a pair of my dad's sweatpants, and her slippers. She was in the kitchen preparing dinner, humming some song with a heavy alto vibrato. Being that our space was so small, both the living room and the kitchen were nestled next to each other. I watched my mom as she gently placed a flour-coated chicken wing in the hot grease with a few other pieces that were already in the pan as she continued to hum and sing under her breath. The grease popped and fizzled. "This is my story; this is my song. Praising my savior all the day long …"

I sat and attempted to do my homework, but while I sat there, I was having a really hard time focusing. No matter how hard I tried, I couldn't seem to focus and move past math problem number eight. Something was on my heart. I wanted to share it, but it was too horrible of a secret to share.

I quickly closed my math textbook and switched to my English homework, hoping that the change would help provide a much-needed distraction. It didn't work. I still couldn't focus.

I couldn't hold it in any longer, and I had to tell my secret to someone I trusted, my mom. But when I tried to find the words to tell her, I couldn't find them. So I sat in silence, pondering what I would say as I stared at my English textbook. I finally spoke up, but instead of telling my mom my secret, I asked her a question. "Mom, do you love me?"

My mom with her back to me was still frying chicken. She interrupted her humming and gave the answer most moms would give: "Of course, baby. I love you." She pulled a few of the hot wings from the pan and rested them on some paper towel to soak up the excess grease.

I wasn't satisfied. I needed to be sure that my mom would still love me no matter what my secret was. I asked her again. "Mom, do you love me?"

This time she gave a quick glance over her shoulder and said, "I will always love you. You're my baby." She smiled as she dropped more wings in the flour.

Still fearful and unsatisfied, I attempted to ask her again. This time, my question was unexpectedly cut short. "Mom, do you ..."

I couldn't hold the tears back any longer. My head fell, and I cried hard and bitterly. My mom heard my crying, turned off the stove, quickly wiped her hands, sat next to me, moving my textbooks out of the way, and held me warmly in her arms. Her clothes smelled like perfume and fried chicken. It was exactly what I needed. She didn't say anything. She just let me cry in her arms. It was a very cleansing moment. Finally, a safe space to let go of all the baggage. After a while, I calmed down.

When she noticed I was starting to calm down, she started to speak.

"What's going on, honey? I started to think something was wrong when you kept asking if I loved you. You know I will always love you no matter what. What's wrong?"

"If I tell you, you promise you'll still love me?"

"Baby, you can tell me anything. I will always love you."

She continued to hold me.

I paused for a long while. I was afraid of what my mom's response was going to be.

I finally found the courage to tell my mom what I had to hold onto for so many years. "I think I like boys." I was ashamed, embarrassed, and confused.

My mom grew silent.

"Why do you think you like boys?" Her voice was still tender.

I shrugged my shoulders.

"Do you think you like boys because of what happened between you and Barry on his grandmom's porch?"

I shook my head yes.

This was the first time we spoke in-depth about my traumatic experience beneath the chair on the porch. The more we spoke, the better I began to feel.

My mom realized that it wasn't that I actually liked boys, but instead, I was having a hard time navigating and sorting through a traumatic experience that I thought defined me.

"Well, baby. I don't think that means you like boys. Even though Barry did what he did, it doesn't mean that *you* like boys. There's some stuff that Barry will have to work out when he gets older, but that has nothing to do with you."

"Can I tell you something else?" she offered softly.

"Yes," I said.

"It wasn't your fault, and you don't have nothing to be ashamed of. Don't be mad or angry at Barry. We should pray for him. What he did was wrong, but he was probably acting out something that had happened to him by another boy or one of his family members."

"Okay?"

"Okay. Can I check on you from time to time to see how you're doing?"

"Yes."

"Okay. And we'll keep this between us."

"Okay," I said with a smile. I was feeling better having told my mom what I had been holding onto.

"Can I tell you something else, sweetie?"

I nodded my head yes.

"You can tell me anything. I will *always* love you."

Kind Reminder
Heart Vomit

AFTER YEARS OF swallowing stories and memories, our hearts can become nauseous. Hearts vomit too.

Fresh Coffee

EVERY FEW DAYS, my dad would bring home some little knickknack or broken gadget. He loved gadgets and fixing things. Clocks, vacuum cleaners, and radios. He even brought home a microwave he had found. Thingamabobs, whatchamacallits, doohickies, doodads, thingamajigs, gizmos, whatnots, and thingummies frequently passed through the threshold of our door.

One day, I was sitting in my usual place in the living room doing my homework, and my mom was in the kitchen getting ready to prepare dinner. We heard keys jingling at the door. The door swung open. It was my dad. He had just got home from work. He was holding his lunch bag in one hand and a long LED screen in the other. My mom and I looked at each other. The words *Fresh Coffee* darted across the screen in red letters.

I already knew what was getting ready to happen. In

my head, I heard, "Ding, ding, ding, let's get ready to rumble!" Then it started.

"No," my mom said firmly.

"No? No, what?" my dad asked.

"What do you mean, 'no, what?' You know what I'm saying no to. No to that sign you're holding in your hand." *Fresh Coffee* sped across the screen again.

"Honey, it's a sign. We can change the words on it and everything."

"What do we need a sign that says, 'Fresh Coffee' for?"

I sat quietly as I watched to see who would win this match. Usually, it was my mom. My eyes bounced from left to right as I watched each of my parents serve the next response.

"Honey, we can change the words on it. It can give the date and time and everything!" he said, fumbling with the back of the sign to do just that. *Fresh Coffee* sped across again.

"Nope. We don't need it. It's junk. Get rid of it."

My dad stood at the door, defeated by the reigning champ. He dropped his lunch bag on the sofa and carried the sign to the trash.

Fresh Coffee sped past again.

Kind Reminder
Corns and Calluses

CALLUS (N.) CAL-US | ka-les

Calluses are thick, hardened layers of skin that develop when your skin tries to protect itself against friction and pressure.

Hearts need exfoliating too.

Poop on the Sidewalk

IT WAS 3:00 p.m., and the bell had just rung, and all the kids in the school stampeded out of the doors and flooded the sidewalks. I was in eighth grade. Kids were screaming, laughing, and trading stories of who had the worst teacher and who had the most homework. It was always noisy around this time. The kids had been away from their friends, listened to boring lectures, and been locked in school all day. This was the first time to be free since the morning bell. I didn't usually stand around with the other kids because I didn't have many friends, so after school, I would head home. It was springtime, and the warm sun hung overhead like a brilliant yellow ornament.

While I was walking home, I was deep in thought, looking at the ground as its bumpy tan skin glided along as I walked. My turtle shell of a bookbag swooshed from side to side with each step I took. My bookbag was usually heavy. I had intentionally left some of my textbooks at school the week prior so, when I got home, I wouldn't be able to do my homework and I could watch television. My mom caught on and started making me bring home every textbook my teachers gave me. Even if I didn't have homework in a certain class. While I was walking, I felt a tug on my bookbag. I snapped out of my daydream and whirled around to see who had grabbed my bookbag. It was my friend Tiffany. Tiffany was amazing. She had long black hair that grew past her shoulders that she always pulled back into a ponytail. She never carried her books in her book bag. She always carried them in her arms close to her chest as if she was hugging them with her head held high as if she was sniffing the air. She was one of the cool kids who knew everyone. Everyone knew not to mess with her because she had an older brother that most of the other kids were afraid of. Even though she was one of the cool kids, somehow, she befriended me. Her friendship made me feel less like an alien and almost normal. Even though I didn't blend in with the other kids, she made me feel like I mattered. She had so much confidence and always smiled.

"Hey, Tommie! You going home?" she said loudly. She was always loud.

"Hey, Tif! Yeah, Ms. Robbins told us we had to do all the math problems in chapter 7. I hate her class."

"Yeah, I have her third period. I never understand what she's talking about."

We both laughed.

On our way home, we talked about the teachers we

liked and the teachers we hated. Tiffany didn't live too far from me. Usually, when we reached Old York Road, we parted ways.

While we were walking home and talking about school and the kids in our class, Tiffany changed the subject.

"Tommie."

"Hmm?"

"Can I ask you a question?"

"Yeah. What's up?"

"Why do you always look down when you walk?"

I didn't have an answer. I didn't know that I looked down when I walked.

"I don't know. I guess so I can see where I'm walking. I'm not trying to step in dookie." I tried to laugh it off. Tiffany didn't laugh.

"Yeah, but you look down *all* the time. There ain't that much poop on the ground, Tommie. So you only look down to see poop?"

When she asked it this way, it made my reason for looking down sound really poor.

"I don't know. I just always look down at the ground."

"Well, it doesn't look good when you look down. It makes you look sad or like you're afraid of people. If people see you look down, they'll try to chump you. When you look up, it makes you look confident. So look up, okay?"

"Okay," I said with a shy grin, trying to hide my smile.

I needed to hear that. She was right; I wasn't looking at the ground to avoid stepping in poop.

Kind Reminder
The Truth About Healing

The truth is that healing can be a wild, unpredictable, amazing, uncomfortable, messy, enlightening, fragile, painful, sweet, and ugly process. But that's what makes it beautiful.

War

OOM. A FLASH of orange and yellow fire followed by dark clouds of smoke blossom and bloom like tall flowers in the distance. A bomb just exploded. Tanks crawl over corpses with their metal feet leaving tracks everywhere.

Bodies, faces, lifeless. These were sons, these were daughters, these were spouses, fathers, and mothers. Eyes once full of life now turned cold, dark, empty, and abandoned. A warm home, now a cold abode.

The scent of flesh crisping and burning fills my nostril. I try not to gag. The rapid fire of machine guns and orders being screamed fills the afternoon air. At least I think it's afternoon. I lost track. We've been in this same battle since yesterday. Still no white flags. No surrender. No peace. The battle rages on.

The battles that are the most difficult to fight are the

ones that no one sees. Like the ones that happen in the mind or heart.

Kind Reminder
Accidental Ventriloquists

OUR HEARTS ARE not dummies, puppets, or some lifeless object. They are alive. They are intelligent. They are aware. They have a voice. Learning to stop speaking for them and start listening to them is one of the greatest gifts we can give ourselves.

Summertime

IT WAS SUMMER. The school year had ended, and all the kids in the neighborhood were on summer break. Occasionally, some of us went down south to visit family or went to Disney if their family had money, but usually, we all stayed home in the neighborhood. I would normally stay in the house and watch television, but sometimes I would go out and hang with the kids on the block and enjoy the summer weather. When I was a kid, summer wasn't just a season with a blazing sun and hot weather. It was an experience. One of the hidden gems that made living in a big city not feel so bad.

Summer had a rhythm like the clapping of the white jump rope slapping the black street between parked cars as girls giggled and laughed while they played Double Dutch.

Summer tasted like the sweet nectar we found in white

and yellow honeysuckles that we plucked from a nearby fence in the driveway next to the abandoned car.

Summer was ten ashy and scuffed sneakers gathered together in a circle while one of us chanted "Doggy Doggy Diamond" to see who would have to count for Freeze Tag.

"Just because you kissed the girl behind the magazine."

Summer was "you better have your butt in this house before the street lights come on, and you better not leave the block."

Summer was the sound of the music playing from the Mr. Softee Ice Cream truck as it drove down the street with black and brown kids chasing it with balled-up dollars in hand.

Summer felt like vanilla and chocolate ice cream swirls dripping between our fingers, down our chins, and down our grins.

Summer was sweet like jawbreakers, Swedish Fish, Now-Laters (not Now and Laters), Air Heads, peanut chews, hugs, sunflower seeds, Dip Stix, Moon Pies, grape popsicles, and purple tongues.

Summer was running through the cool water of a fire hydrant because we couldn't afford pools.

Summer was the gunshots that fired a few blocks away. I wish I didn't live here.

"Tommie, get your butt in this house!"

The Sexton's Son

"TOMMIE ... TOMMIE ... TOMMIE ... wake up, honey." It was my mom standing next to my bed. It was two o'clock in the morning, and she was barely awake herself. My bed was warm and soft beneath the thick tan blanket, and I had no plans of waking up before the sun. The welcomed darkness in my room was interrupted by the light from the hallway from my door my mom had opened to wake me up.

"Mmmmmmm," I said groggily. I turned over and nestled beneath the warmth of my blanket even more. "Come on, honey. Get up. Your dad is at the church, and he needs our help cleaning it."

"Okaaaay." I wanted to tell her to leave me alone, but I knew better.

I hated cleaning the church. Not only was I forced to get out of my warm bed to vacuum and clean bathrooms, but I also felt a little embarrassed that my family had to clean the church. Other kids and families who attended the church knew about it. No matter what, we worked together to keep the lights on. At one time, we even cleaned movie theaters. We would wait until the last movie finished playing before we started sweeping up popcorn and tossing cups filled with ice and soda.

In the middle of my tenth-grade year, the church we were attending had purchased a new church building, which also included two houses, one on either side. The church decided to rent one of the houses to my family, and in return, my dad agreed to serve as the church's sexton. A sexton is similar to a janitor or groundskeeper. While my dad served as a sexton, he was also a truck driver who wouldn't get off until 2:00 a.m. Normally, he would drop the truck off and then go right into cleaning the church. He would sometimes only get two to three hours of sleep before he had to wake up again to drive the truck.

Barely coherent, I threw on a pair of gray sweatpants lying nearby at the bottom of my bed, a light blue hoodie, and some old sneakers and headed next door to the church. I grabbed the multipurpose cleaner, mirror cleaner, bleach, and toilet cleaner from the janitor's closet to scrub the toilets, collect trash, and clean the bathroom sinks. My mom helped clean too. She and I usually had the easy stuff. My dad did the most difficult jobs like cleaning the sanctuary and the large rooms, mopping, and buffing the floors.

When I was finished and vacuumed the last hallway,

I went to go find my dad to tell him I had finished and was heading back to the house. Sometimes it was hard to find him because I didn't know which room he was cleaning in. This particular day, I found him easily. I followed the distant monotone hum of the high-powered floor buffer until it became louder. When I found him, he was exhausted. He was leaning over the large floor buffer machine, eyes barely open, using the remaining strength he had to sway the buffer from side to side.

"Hey, dad. You okay?"

"Tommie-o! Yeah, son, I'm okay. You done?"

"Yeah, I'm done. I'm heading back to the house."

"Okay, thanks for helping your dad out. I really appreciate it. Go and get some sleep."

As soon as he relieved me of my duty, I hugged him and disappeared behind the exit door to head home.

Kind Reminder
Life Carriers

We all possess a divine ability to carry and birth life. Yes, men have wombs too.

Blow It Out Your ...

I HAD JUST GOTTEN my permit and was still learning to navigate tight turns, negotiate the distance between my car and an oncoming car, and just get comfortable behind the wheel. Learning how to drive in Philadelphia was quite an experience that caused me a lot of anxiety. Philadelphia drivers are always in a rush, quick tempered, and remorseless.

My mom and I had just finished running our last errand for the day and were walking back toward the car to head home, bags in hand, when my mom called to me.

"Hey."

"Huh," I responded.

"Here, you're driving us home," she said with a grin, tossing me the keys.

Smiling, I caught the keys and hopped in the driver's seat.

"Okay, so you remember how to do this, right? Adjust

the seat and your mirrors and take your time. When you pull out the spot, go slow, take your time, and check your mirrors," my mom said.

"Okay," I said, smiling while adjusting the rearview mirror. I felt like such an adult being in the driver's seat. Her wisdom was overshadowed by my excitement.

I pulled the car out of the parking spot without any issues. That was easy enough. But driving home wasn't easy at all. The entire time I was beyond nervous, constantly checking the mirrors and trying to stay in my lane. My hands gripped the steering wheel tightly to make sure the car kept its course while my foot barely pressed the gas pedal. We were driving very slowly. In fact, we were driving below the speed limit.

"That's it," my mom reassured me. "Take your time. We ain't in no rush."

I nodded, only semicomforted by my mom's words; the nervousness was still very present.

We made it up to Old Stenton before you get to Germantown Avenue and Berkley Street, which takes you to Seventy-Six. On one corner of Old Stenton stood a small church, and on the other corner was an apartment complex. Around this area, cars sped and barely stopped at the stop sign. Cars zipped and zoomed without a second thought or regret.

After a few successful turns, I was starting to get a little more comfortable behind the wheel. Suddenly, something shattered my fragile new driver's confidence. Car horns.

The car horns behind me screamed, blared, and blasted. Immediately, I panicked. My heart raced, and I grabbed the steering wheel so tight my palms ached from my fingers digging into them as they wrapped around the wheel. The cars behind me didn't care that I was scared, that I was still learning to drive, or that beeping their horns made me more nervous. They wanted me to drive faster or move out of the way.

My mom sensed my uneasiness and shared some advice with me that I would never have expected to hear from her. I guess she got tired of all the horn honking that was clearly my fault for being such a horrible, novice driver.

She yelled out, "Oh, blow it out your butt!"

My eyes widened, and my head snapped to look at my mom sitting in the passenger seat. I have never heard my mom say anything like that. This was the woman who had me in church every Sunday, made me say my prayers every evening, and wouldn't allow me to say that I hated anyone.

"Tommie, don't worry about them. I'm sorry. I know I shouldn't have said that, but they're gonna have to wait. You take your time, baby, and anyone who doesn't like it can blow it out their butts. Yes, I said it. Now drive."

The horns continued to beep, and my driving didn't improve, but my mom's comment made a lot of the uneasiness dissipate. My mom and I laughed all the way home.

And anyone who doesn't like it can blow it out their butts.

Cookies and Crumbs

MY MOM AND I decided to hang out one evening at one of our favorite restaurants, which was near where she lived. We always enjoyed going to that restaurant. The staff was always pleasant and warm, and the ambiance was always just right. Music never played in this place, but the dim lights and the chatter from other tables made for a perfect dining experience.

"Please follow me, Mr. Suggs." We wanted a booth, but we were seated at a small table. We both were too hungry to care or wait longer for a booth. We searched the menu for whatever caught our attention and devoured the complimentary bread and butter they provide. My mom ordered salmon, and I ordered seafood pasta. The food was delicious. The alfredo sauce served with my seafood pasta was perfect. My mom also seemed to thoroughly enjoy her food.

While we were eating, we spent our time catching

up and recalling old memories that always started with, "Remember when ..." Usually, the story that followed always made us laugh. We would have to quiet ourselves so the people dining near us wouldn't be annoyed. Sometimes, the stories would be so funny we would laugh into our napkins.

The laughter from the previous "remember when" story was starting to quiet down when my mom asked me, "So what was it like growing up for you?" I felt the energy of the conversation shift almost like a rip current dragging me unexpectedly further into the ocean of conversation I wasn't prepared to have.

"What do you mean?" I asked.

I knew exactly what she meant. It was a question that I had given a lot of thought to, but I never openly shared my feelings about my upbringing with anyone. Her question required transparency and vulnerability, which can be uncomfortable.

She didn't back down. "I want to know what it was like for you growing up in our household when you were younger."

I sat quietly for a moment because I didn't know how to answer this question.

The silverware clanging against the glass plates and the banter from the other tables became more noticeable in my silence. I stared at one of the last remaining pieces of shrimp on my plate with a few noodles laying near it as I pondered my answer. I wanted to be honest, but I wasn't sure how honest I was supposed to be. I also knew I couldn't lie because my mom wanted to know the truth.

"Well, honestly, there were some good times and some hard times. Like when you and Grammy surprised me and Cam with a trip to Disney World. That was my first time flying on an airplane. We had so much fun! I wanted waffles for dinner, and Cam wanted spaghetti for breakfast. I'll never forget that trip."

My mom laughed. "Yeah, that was a lot of fun. You didn't know what was going on when you got on that plane."

"So what about the hard times?" She asked. She cut through me wanting to focus on the positive. She wanted the truth.

I obliged. While I spoke, my mom sat quietly and nodded.

I kept sharing and talking about what it was like for me growing up. The more I shared, the more comfortable I became with sharing thoughts that were very personal. But in the middle of sharing, I stopped.

"What's wrong?" She asked. "Why did you stop?"

I sat a little longer without saying anything and stared at my mom quietly.

I interrupted my silence. "Thank you."

"Thank you? For what?" I could see that she was puzzled.

"Mom, thank you for everything you have done for

me. While I was speaking, a lightbulb went off. I realized that even though there were some difficulties growing up, you ate the cookie."

"Ate the cookie? What does that mean?" I could tell she was becoming more confused.

"Yeah, you ate the cookie. Basically, all the harsh realities that surrounded us you swallowed and ate so I wouldn't have to. You did everything in your power to make sure I was protected, safe, and happy. I'm over here complaining about crumbs, but you ate the cookie. Even though you couldn't protect me from everything, you ate the cookie. I can't complain about a few crumbs. I can't even imagine what it was like for you and dad taking on all that reality and responsibility and not only shielding me from it but trying to make sure I didn't see it."

Her eyes filled up with tears. She understood the analogy.

"Baby, we did the best we could." Her tears started to fall.

"I didn't know you still saw me and your dad struggle so bad. We tried to keep you from it so you could grow up in a safe and happy home."

My eyes started to swell with tears partly because of the tears running down my mom's cheek. It's hard for me to see my mom cry. The main reason my eyes started to swell, however, was because I realized that the same stories and events that were hard for me to experience were also hard for them, but I had been so engulfed in my own narrative that I could not see them. I only saw myself. My story wasn't my story at all. It was shared and consisted of other people who also felt frustration, fear, confusion, worry, and a bunch of God whys. Our conversation allowed me to see the story from a larger context.

We ended our conversation with me again expressing much gratitude for everything they had done. We paid the check and left the restaurant to go home.

Mom and Dad, I finally see you. Thanks for eating the cookie.

Kind Reminder
Retinas

I F WE ONLY see with our eyes, we won't see much at all. But if we allow ourselves to see with our hearts, we may see things much clearer. Our hearts have retinas.

Kind Reminder
Heavy Ink

S OME OF OUR stories carry so much weight that the very ink used to write them feels heavy.

Nevertheless, we are the spine of our own book and have been graced to carry the volume of our pages. We're stronger than we think.